SIDE-SPLITTING

KNOCK-KNOCK JOKES for kids

BOB PHILLIPS

HARVEST HOUSE PUBLISHERS
EUGENE, OREGON

Cover by Dugan Design Group, Bloomington, Minnesota

SIDE-SPLITTING KNOCK-KNOCK JOKES FOR KIDS
Copyright © 2012 by Bob Phillips
Published by Harvest House Publishers
Eugene, Oregon 97402
www.harvesthousepublishers.com

ISBN 978-0-7369-4836-4 (pbk.)
ISBN 978-0-7369-4837-1 (eBook)

Printed in the United States of America

15 16 17 18 19 / BP-NI / 10 9 8 7

CONTENTS

1

DON'T KICK THE DOOR IN!

Knock, knock.
Who's there?
Area.
Area who?
Area deaf? Can't you hear me knocking?

Knock, knock.
Who's there?
Belinda.
Belinda who?
Belinda or not, it's me.

Knock, knock.
Who's there?
Cat.
Cat who?
Cat you see I'm busy?

Knock, knock.
Who's there?
Dandelion.
Dandelion who?
Dandelion is a very well-dressed lion.

Knock, knock.
Who's there?
Evans.
Evans who?
Evans you gotten tired of these jokes yet?

Knock, knock.
Who's there?
Gorilla.
Gorilla who?
The Gorilla your dreams.

Knock, knock.
Who's there?
Harmony.
Harmony who?
Harmony knock-knock jokes would you like to hear?

Knock, knock.
Who's there?
Iowa.
Iowa who?
Iowa lot of money—how about you?

Knock, knock.
Who's there?
Juliet.
Juliet who?
Juliet pancakes for breakfast.

Knock, knock.
Who's there?
Kent.
Kent who?
Kent come out and play right now.

Knock, knock.
Who's there?
Lana.
Lana who?
Lana on my feet.

Knock, knock.
Who's there?
Noah.
Noah who?
I Noah lot more knock-knock jokes!

Knock, knock.
Who's there?
Ozzie.
Ozzie who?
Ozzie you later, alligator!

Knock, knock.
Who's there?
Pencil.
Pencil who?
Your Pencil fall down if you lose too much weight.

Knock, knock.
Who's there?
Selma.
Selma who?
I'll Selma old soccer ball for five dollars.

Knock, knock.
Who's there?
Thermos.
Thermos who?
Thermos be some way to get you to open the door!

Knock, knock.
Who's there?
Viper.
Viper who?
Viper feet—your shoes are muddy.

Knock, knock.
Who's there?
Wendell.
Wendell who?
Wendell you let me in?

Knock, knock.
Who's there?
Yvonne.
Yvonne who?
Yvonne to go on a date?

Knock, knock.
Who's there?
Zink.
Zink who?
Just Zink—I could tell you knock-knock jokes all day!

2

YOU'VE GOT THE WRONG HOUSE!

Knock, knock.
Who's there?
Aria.
Aria who?
Aria tired of hearing knock-knock jokes?

Knock, knock.
Who's there?
Butcher.
Butcher who?
Butcher best foot forward.

Knock, knock.
Who's there?
Coffin.
Coffin who?
I'm Coffin a lot because of this cold.

Knock, knock.
Who's there?
Deceit.
Deceit who?
Deceit of my pants has a hole in it.

Knock, knock.
Who's there?
Eduora.
Eduora who?
Eduora squeaks when it opens.

Knock, knock.
Who's there?
Fleece.
Fleece who?
Fleece open the door!

Knock, knock.
Who's there?
Gargoyle.
Gargoyle who?
Gargoyle with mouthwash and your breath will smell
    better.

Knock, knock.
Who's there?
Hatch-hatch-hatch.
Hatch-hatch-hatch who?
Do you have a cold?

Knock, knock.
Who's there?
Ima.
Ima who?
Ima glad you like knock-knock jokes.

Knock, knock.
Who's there?
Kiefer.
Kiefer who?
The Kiefer this door must be here somewhere...

Knock, knock.
Who's there?
Lacey.
Lacey who?
Lacey your shoes—they're untied.

Knock, knock.
Who's there?
Musket.
Musket who?
I Musket a new joke book quick!

Knock, knock.
Who's there?
Omelet.
Omelet who?
Omelet happier reading this book.

Knock, knock.
Who's there?
Pecan.
Pecan who?
Pecan the window to see if he's there.

Knock, knock.
Who's there?
Rudy.
Hey, I'm Rudy!
Aw, c'mon—don't be Rudy to me!

Knock, knock.
Who's there?
Sherwood.
Sherwood who?
Sherwood like to have you open the door.

Knock, knock.
Who's there?
Turnip.
Turnip who?
Turnip the heat and let me in—I'm freezing.

Knock, knock.
Who's there?
Ven.
Ven who?
Ven you let me in, I'll tell you.

Knock, knock.
Who's there?
Wanda.
Wanda who?
Wanda go to the movies?

Knock, knock.
Who's there?
You.
You who?
Did you call?

Knock, knock.
Who's there?
Zany.
Zany who?
Zany body home?

3

TRY USING A KEY!

Knock, knock.
Who's there?
Atom.
Atom who?
Atom bomb. (That joke blew up.)

Knock, knock.
Who's there?
Carmen.
Carmen who?
Carmen get your dinner.

Knock, knock.
Who's there?
Diana.
Diana who?
I'm Diana hunger from standing out here so long.

Knock, knock.
Who's there?
Event.
Event who?
Event away and left me alone.

Knock, knock.
Who's there?
Forest.
Forest who?
Forest the number before five.

Knock, knock.
Who's there?
Gibbon.
Gibbon who?
Are you Gibbon me a hard time?

Knock, knock.
Who's there?
Icing.
Icing who?
Icing in the school choir.

Knock, knock.
Who's there?
Jewel.
Jewel who?
Jewel never know until you open the door.

Knock, knock.
Who's there?
Leaf.
Leaf who?
Leaf me outside much longer and I'll freeze!

Knock, knock.
Who's there?
Maura.
Maura who?
Maura knock-knock jokes will drive me crazy!

Knock, knock.
Who's there?
Norma Lee.
Norma Lee who?
Norma Lee I would tell you, but not today.

Knock, knock.
Who's there?
Popeye.
Popeye who?
Popeye need the car tonight, okay?

Knock, knock.
Who's there?
Raptor.
Raptor who?
She Raptor hula hoop around her hips.

Knock, knock.
Who's there?
Sonia.
Sonia who?
Sonia matter of time before I kick the door down.

Knock, knock.
Who's there?
Torch.
Torch who?
Torch you would never ask.

Knock, knock.
Who's there?
Vasha.
Vasha who?
Vasha your dirty hands!

Knock, knock.
Who's there?
Wendy.
Wendy who?
Wendy day, isn't it?

Knock, knock.
Who's there?
Yvette.
Yvette who?
Yvette might help your sickly pet.

Knock, knock.
Who's there?
Zinging.
Zinging who?
I'm Zinging a happy song!

4
I'M ALL KNOCKED OUT!

Knock, knock.
Who's there?
Avenue.
Avenue who?
Avenue heard me knocking?

Knock, knock.
Who's there?
Board.
Board who?
I'm Board to death waiting for you to open the door!

Knock, knock.
Who's there?
Cattle.
Cattle who?
A Cattle always look for mice.

Knock, knock.
Who's there?
Diesel.
Diesel who?
Diesel be a funny knock-knock joke.

Knock, knock.
Who's there?
Eiffel.
Eiffel who?
Eiffel down and skinned my knee.

Knock, knock.
Who's there?
Friar.
Friar who?
Friar up some hamburgers and hot dogs.

Knock, knock.
Who's there?
Gertie.
Gertie who?
Gertie is better than my tea.

Knock, knock.
Who's there?
Harvey.
Harvey who?
Harvey ever going to get into your house?

Knock, knock.
Who's there?
Ivanna.
Ivanna who?
Ivanna hold your hand.

Knock, knock.
Who's there?
Jacket.
Jacket who?
Jacket the store said you would like this.

Knock, knock.
Who's there?
Kristin.
Kristin who?
Kristin a new boat by breaking a bottle on it.

Knock, knock.
Who's there?
Lettuce.
Lettuce who?
Lettuce in and you'll see.

Knock, knock.
Who's there?
Mikey.
Mikey who?
Mikey won't work in the lock.

Knock, knock.
Who's there?
Neil.
Neil who?
Neil down before the king!

Knock, knock.
Who's there?
Picture.
Picture who?
I Picture door out and thought I'd knock on it.

Knock, knock.
Who's there?
Raisin.
Raisin who?
Raisin chickens is cheep work.

Knock, knock.
Who's there?
Shaver.
Shaver who?
Shaver face—it's getting hairy.

Knock, knock.
Who's there?
Tennis.
Tennis who?
Tennis the number that comes before eleven.

Knock, knock.
Who's there?
Viper.
Viper who?
Viper nose—it's running.

Knock, knock.
Who's there?
Walter.
Walter who?
Walter you asking so many questions for?

Knock, knock.
Who's there?
Yukon.
Yukon who?
Yukon lead a horse to water, but you can't make him
    drink!

Knock, knock.
Who's there?
Zoom.
Zoom who?
Zoom did you expect?

WHO'S THUMPING ON MY DOOR?

Knock, knock.
Who's there?
Axe.
Axe who?
Axe me to tell another knock-knock joke.

Knock, knock.
Who's there?
Bee.
Bee who?
Bee polite and let me come in.

Knock, knock.
Who's there?
Culver.
Culver who?
Culver up my head—I'm getting a sunburn.

Knock, knock.
Who's there?
Dish Towel.
Dish Towel who?
Dish Towel is soaked—it fell in the swimming pool.

Knock, knock.
Who's there?
Exam.
Exam who?
Exam bacon make a great breakfast!

Knock, knock.
Who's there?
France.
France who?
My France and I play ball during recess.

Knock, knock.
Who's there?
Gladys.
Gladys who?
Gladys summer vacation—how about you?

Knock, knock.
Who's there?
Hannover.
Hannover who?
Hannover the keys or open the door!

Knock, knock.
Who's there?
Iguana.
Iguana who?
Iguana hold your hand.

Knock, knock.
Who's there?
Juno.
Juno who?
Juno any other knock-knock jokes?

Knock, knock.
Who's there?
Kelp.
Kelp who?
Kelp me—I'm drowning!

Knock, knock.
Who's there?
Marionette.
Marionette who?
Marionette all the cake and didn't leave any for us.

Knock, knock.
Who's there?
Piggyback.
Piggyback who?
Piggyback into the fan and now has no tail to tell.

Knock, knock.
Who's there?
Robin.
Robin who?
Robin people will land you in jail.

Knock, knock.
Who's there?
Theresa.
Theresa who?
Theresa fly in my soup!

Knock, knock.
Who's there?
Venice.
Venice who?
Venice he going to be done with these knock-knock
  jokes?

Knock, knock.
Who's there?
Wound.
Wound who?
Wound you please let me in?

Knock, knock.
Who's there?
Yukon.
Yukon who?
Yukon say that again.

I'LL KNOCK-KNOCK YOUR DOOR DOWN!

Knock, knock.
Who's there?
Ali.
Ali who?
Ali, Ali, oxen free.

Knock, knock.
Who's there?
Bear.
Bear who?
Bear, oh Bear has my little dog gone?

Knock, knock.
Who's there?
Celeste.
Celeste who?
This is Celeste time I'm coming to your house!

Knock, knock.
Who's there?
Doctor Dolittle.
Doctor Dolittle who?
Doctor Dolittle with my broken finger—it still hurts.

Knock, knock.
Who's there?
Eclipse.
Eclipse who?
Eclipse my toenails.

Knock, knock.
Who's there?
Fiddle.
Fiddle who?
Fiddle secrets are hard to keep.

Knock, knock.
Who's there?
Hawaii.
Hawaii who?
Fine, thanks. Hawaii you?

Knock, knock.
Who's there?
Irish Stew.
Irish Stew who?
Irish Stew would let me tell you a few more knock-
knock jokes.

Knock, knock.
Who's there?
Judy.
Judy who?
Judy liver my Krispy Kreme doughnuts?

Knock, knock.
Who's there?
Kenya.
Kenya who?
Kenya please let me in?

Knock, knock.
Who's there?
Lion.
Lion who?
I'm Lion on the beach to get a tan.

Knock, knock.
Who's there?
Missouri.
Missouri who?
Missouri loves company.

Knock, knock.
Who's there?
Pizza.
Pizza who?
I'd like to give him a Pizza my mind!

Knock, knock.
Who's there?
Ron.
Ron who?
Ron fast and open the door!

Knock, knock.
Who's there?
Seymour.
Seymour who?
I Seymour bad weather is coming.

Knock, knock.
Who's there?
Tilly.
Tilly who?
Let's Tilly ground and plant some flowers.

Knock, knock.
Who's there?
Vaughan.
Vaughan who?
Vaughan day I'll run out of these jokes!

Knock, knock.
Who's there?
Weirdo.
Weirdo who?
Weirdo you think you're going?

Knock, knock.
Who's there?
Yah.
Yah who?
I didn't know you were a cowboy!

7

YOU'RE KNOCKING A HOLE IN MY DOOR!

Knock, knock.
Who's there?
Adair.
Adair who?
Adair you to open the door and find out.

Knock, knock.
Who's there?
Bacon.
Bacon who?
I'm Bacon a cherry pie for your party.

Knock, knock.
Who's there?
Coal Mine.
Coal Mine who?
Coal Mine friends, and they'll tell you who I am.

Knock, knock.
Who's there?
Dallas.
Dallas who?
Dallas in Wonderland.

Knock, knock.
Who's there?
Eileen Dover.
Eileen Dover who?
Eileen Dover and fell on my nose.

Knock, knock.
Who's there?
Fleece.
Fleece who?
Fleece are biting your dog!

Knock, knock.
Who's there?
Howie.
Howie who?
Howie 'bout going for a walk?

Knock, knock.
Who's there?
Knotting.
Knotting who?
Knotting ventured, knotting gained.

Knock, knock.
Who's there?
Liver.
Liver who?
You know, Ida Liver...

Knock, knock.
Who's there?
Marietta.
Marietta who?
Marietta a big bowl of ice cream.

Knock, knock.
Who's there?
Omelet and Butter.
Omelet and Butter who?
Omelet smarter than you so you Butter open the door.

Knock, knock.
Who's there?
Poodle.
Poodle who?
Poodle little love in your heart.

Knock, knock.
Who's there?
Salad.
Salad who?
Salad a wonderful time at your party.

Knock, knock.
Who's there?
Terrace.
Terrace who?
Terrace a fly in my soup!

Knock, knock.
Who's there?
Vault.
Vault who?
Vault sing Matilda, Vault sing Matilda...

Knock, knock.
Who's there?
Weird.
Weird who?
Weird you get such a funny face?

Knock, knock.
Who's there?
Your mom.
Your mom who?
Very funny. Now let me in.

8

STOP WHACKING ON MY DOOR!

Knock, knock.
Who's there?
Athena.
Athena who?
Athena flying thauther.

Knock, knock.
Who's there?
Bear Skin.
Bear Skin who?
Bear Skin climb trees.

Knock, knock.
Who's there?
Clare.
Clare who?
Clare out of the way—I'm comin' in!

Knock, knock.
Who's there?
Despair.
Despair who?
Despair of shoes is too tight!

Knock, knock.
Who's there?
Era.
Era who?
Did you Era knock at the door?

Knock, knock.
Who's there?
Hammer.
Hammer who?
Would you like Hammer bacon with those eggs?

Knock, knock.
Who's there?
Iran.
Iran who?
Iran a long way to see you.

Knock, knock.
Who's there?
Jamaica.
Jamaica who?
Jamaica lunch for me today?

Knock, knock.
Who's there?
Kansas.
Kansas who?
Kansas be the way to get in?

Knock, knock.
Who's there?
Lois.
Lois who?
The Lois man on the totem pole.

Knock, knock.
Who's there?
Fillmore.
Fillmore who?
We Fillmore bowls of cereal than we can eat.

Knock, knock.
Who's there?
Oslo.
Oslo who?
Oslo down after running a mile.

Knock, knock.
Who's there?
Psalm.
Psalm who?
Psalm day I'll get my own house.

Knock, knock.
Who's there?
Rhona.
Rhona who?
Rhona 'round the race track.

Knock, knock.
Who's there?
Snot.
Snot who?
Snot any of your business.

Knock, knock.
Who's there?
Trader.
Trader who?
Trader Joe's is my favorite store.

Knock, knock.
Who's there?
Worm.
Worm who?
Worm in here, isn't it?

Knock, knock.
Who's there?
Yuma.
Yuma who?
Yuma very funny-looking person.

9

WHAT'S ALL THE BANGING ABOUT?

Knock, knock.
Who's there?
Alfie.
Alfie who?
Alfie better when you finally open the door.

Knock, knock.
Who's there?
Ben and Anna.
Ben and Anna who?
Sad news—Ben and Anna split.

Knock, knock.
Who's there?
Cash.
Cash who?
I always thought you were nuts.

Knock, knock.
Who's there?
Decode.
Decode who?
Decode is in de nose.

Knock, knock.
Who's there?
Everett.
Everett who?
Everett a lizard before?

Knock, knock.
Who's there?
Flo.
Flo who?
Flo, Flo, Flo your boat gently down the stream...

Knock, knock.
Who's there?
Hugh.
Hugh who?
Are you calling me?

Knock, knock.
Who's there?
Irma.
Irma who?
Irma going to keep knocking until you let me in.

Knock, knock.
Who's there?
Jacqueline.
Jacqueline who?
Jacqueline Hyde is a scary story.

Knock, knock.
Who's there?
Lady.
Lady who?
Lady book down, will you?

Knock, knock.
Who's there?
Myth.
Myth who?
Myth me? I myth you too.

Knock, knock.
Who's there?
Ozzie.
Ozzie who?
Ozzie you through the keyhole.

Knock, knock.
Who's there?
Ruthless.
Ruthless who?
Ruthless coming to open the door.

Knock, knock.
Who's there?
Tree.
Tree who?
Tree strikes and you're out!

Knock, knock.
Who's there?
Wayne.
Wayne who?
Wayne are you going to open the door?

Knock, knock.
Who's there?
Your dad.
Your dad who?
Your dad who will ground you if you don't open the
     door.

10

BEAT ON SOME OTHER DOOR!

Knock, knock.
Who's there?
Ascot.
Ascot who?
Ascot what your country can do for you…

Knock, knock.
Who's there?
Beth.
Beth who?
Beth of luck to you.

Knock, knock.
Who's there?
Chester.
Chester who?
He's Chester happy as a clam.

Knock, knock.
Who's there?
Detail.
Detail who?
Detail dat hangs on de horse.

Knock, knock.
Who's there?
Frayda.
Frayda who?
Are you Frayda opening the door?

Knock, knock.
Who's there?
Hiram.
Hiram who?
Hiram fine, how are you?

Knock, knock.
Who's there?
Island.
Island who?
Island on my bottom when I slip off your porch.

Knock, knock.
Who's there?
Lion.
Lion who?
I'm Lion on your porch until you open the door.

Knock, knock.
Who's there?
Mandy.
Mandy who?
Mandy lifeboats, we're sinking!

Knock, knock.
Who's there?
Owl.
Owl who?
Owl be sitting here until you open the door.

Knock, knock.
Who's there?
Poster.
Poster who?
You're Poster remember who's there.

Knock, knock.
Who's there?
Sandal.
Sandal who?
Sandal get in your shoes if you walk on the beach.

Knock, knock.
Who's there?
Tucker.
Tucker who?
Tucker in bed and read her a story.

Knock, knock.
Who's there?
Vassar girl.
Vassar girl who?
Vassar girl like you doing in a place like this?

Knock, knock.
Who's there?
Water.
Water who?
Water you waiting for—open the door and find out!

11

KNOCK YOURSELF SILLY!

Knock, knock.
Who's there?
Agnes.
Agnes who?
Agnes and Topeka and the Santa Fe!

Knock, knock.
Who's there?
Baby.
Baby who?
Baby I'll tell you if you open the door.

Knock, knock.
Who's there?
Candy.
Candy who?
Candy cow jump over the moon?

Knock, knock.
Who's there?
Disguise.
Disguise who?
Disguise making me mad for not opening the door.

Knock, knock.
Who's there?
Ease.
Ease who?
Ease up to you to open the door.

Knock, knock.
Who's there?
Folder.
Folder who?
Folder clothes—your room's a mess!

Knock, knock.
Who's there?
Havana.
Havana who?
Havana go to the store with me?

Knock, knock.
Who's there?
India.
India who?
India pendant thinking will get you far!

Knock, knock.
Who's there?
Joan.
Joan who?
Joan call us, we'll call you.

Knock, knock.
Who's there?
Meaty.
Meaty who?
Meaty your family was lots of fun.

Knock, knock.
Who's there?
Otis.
Otis who?
Otis is a funny book!

Knock, knock.
Who's there?
Pat.
Pat who?
Pat me on the back. I just won a contest!

Knock, knock.
Who's there?
Shuttle.
Shuttle who?
Shuttle the windows—the wind is starting to blow.

Knock, knock.
Who's there?
Whale.
Whale who?
Whale don't just stand there—open the door!

12

DO YOU HAVE A SORE HAND YET?

Knock, knock.
Who's there?
Alistair.
Alistair who?
Alistair at the beautiful sunset.

Knock, knock.
Who's there?
Bat.
Bat who?
Bat you'll never figure it out.

Knock, knock.
Who's there?
Column.
Column who?
I'm Column all my friends on the phone.

Knock, knock.
Who's there?
Driver.
Driver who?
Let's Driver crazy with another knock-knock joke.

Knock, knock.
Who's there?
Elaine.
Elaine who?
Elaine down on the job and got fired.

Knock, knock.
Who's there?
Fletcher.
Fletcher who?
Fletcher hand open the door.

Knock, knock.
Who's there?
Heidi.
Heidi who?
Heidi candy before someone eats it all!

Knock, knock.
Who's there?
Julie.
Julie who?
Julie the key under the mat?

Knock, knock.
Who's there?
Liver.
Liver who?
Liver up and have a good time.

Knock, knock.
Who's there?
Marian.
Marian who?
Marian her little lamb.

Knock, knock.
Who's there?
Olive.
Olive who?
Olive these knock-knock jokes are funny!

Knock, knock.
Who's there?
Police.
Police who?
Police open up the door!

Knock, knock.
Who's there?
Say.
Say who?
Who.

Knock, knock.
Who's there?
Think.
Think who?
Think of all the fun you're having.

Knock, knock.
Who's there?
Who.
Who, who?
What are you—an owl?

13

THAT'S A STRIKING NOISE!

Knock, knock.
Who's there?
Ammo.
Ammo who?
Ammo glad you came to the door!

Knock, knock.
Who's there?
Begonia.
Begonia who?
Begonia pardon, but could you answer the door?

Knock, knock.
Who's there?
Cows.
Cows who?
No, no. Cows go moo.

Knock, knock.
Who's there?
Dawn.
Dawn who?
Dawn do anything I wouldn't do!

Knock, knock.
Who's there?
Ellis.
Ellis who?
Ellis the letter that comes after K.

Knock, knock.
Who's there?
Frieda.
Frieda who?
He Frieda lot of chicken for dinner!

Knock, knock.
Who's there?
Hester.
Hester who?
Hester moment and I'll tell you.

Knock, knock.
Who's there?
Ina.
Ina who?
Ina meeny, miney, moe...

Knock, knock.
Who's there?
Justin.
Justin who?
Justin time for dinner!

Knock, knock.
Who's there?
Maia.
Maia who?
Maia, but you take a long time opening the door.

Knock, knock.
Who's there?
Pushkin.
Pushkin who?
Pushkin people around is not a good idea.

Knock, knock.
Who's there?
Scold.
Scold who?
Scold out here—let me in!

Knock, knock.
Who's there?
Thor.
Thor who?
My knuckleth are Thor from knocking.

14

THREE MORE STRIKES AND YOU'RE OUT!

Knock, knock.
Who's there?
Arletta.
Arletta who?
Arletta people like these knock-knock jokes.

Knock, knock.
Who's there?
Blaine.
Blaine who?
Don't Blaine me for these silly jokes!

Knock, knock.
Who's there?
Coen.
Coen who?
Are you Coen to let me in?

Knock, knock.
Who's there?
Disaster.
Disaster who?
Disaster be my lucky day.

Knock, knock.
Who's there?
Ezra.
Ezra who?
Ezra doctor in the house?

Knock, knock.
Who's there?
Ferry.
Ferry who?
Ferry tales are fun to read.

Knock, knock.
Who's there?
Hammond.
Hammond who?
Let's have Hammond eggs for breakfast!

Knock, knock.
Who's there?
Ice Cream.
Ice Cream who?
Ice Cream if you don't let me in.

Knock, knock.
Who's there?
Luke.
Luke who?
Luke out the window, silly—then you'll know who's here.

Knock, knock.
Who's there?
Margo.
Margo who?
Margo rounds make me dizzy.

Knock, knock.
Who's there?
Olga.
Olga who?
Olga away if you don't open the door.

Knock, knock.
Who's there?
Pudding.
Pudding who?
Are you Pudding me on?

Knock, knock.
Who's there?
Scolder.
Scolder who?
The longer you wait, the Scolder it gets out here.

Knock, knock.
Who's there?
Thumb.
Thumb who?
Thumb day my prince will come.

15

KNOCK OFF ALL THE NOISE!

Knock, knock.
Who's there?
Amos.
Amos who?
Amos be crazy thinking you'll answer the door.

Knock, knock.
Who's there?
Cynthia.
Cynthia who?
Cynthia won't open the door, I'll keep knocking.

Knock, knock.
Who's there?
Dinah.
Dinah who?
Dinah's sore!

Knock, knock.
Who's there?
Evans.
Evans who?
Evans you gotten tired of these jokes yet?

Knock, knock.
Who's there?
Hannah.
Hannah who?
Hannah me a key or open the door!

Knock, knock.
Who's there?
Juan.
Juan who?
Juan day I'll find even more jokes!

Knock, knock.
Who's there?
Leif.
Leif who?
Leif me a key when you lock the door.

Knock, knock.
Who's there?
Minnie.
Minnie who?
Minnie people think knock-knock jokes are crazy.

Knock, knock.
Who's there?
On.
On who?
On the moon, baboon.

Knock, knock.
Who's there?
Phyllis.
Phyllis who?
Phyllis up the car—it's out of gas.

Knock, knock.
Who's there?
Should Hold.
Should Hold who?
"Should Hold acquaintance be forgot…"

Knock, knock.
Who's there?
Torres.
Torres who?
He Torres pants on a nail.

16

POLICE—OPEN UP THE DOOR!

Knock, knock.
Who's there?
Aida.
Aida who?
Aida whole pizza for dinner.

Knock, knock.
Who's there?
Barley.
Barley who?
I Barley know what to say.

Knock, knock.
Who's there?
Cosmonaut.
Cosmonaut who?
Don't ask me, Cosmonaut the one doing all the knocking.

Knock, knock.
Who's there?
Disk.
Disk who?
Disk is a funny book!

Knock, knock.
Who's there?
Eva.
Eva who?
Eva you're deaf, or your doorbell isn't working.

Knock, knock.
Who's there?
Guru.
Guru who?
You Guru six inches since I last saw you.

Knock, knock.
Who's there?
Habit.
Habit who?
Habit you can't guess.

Knock, knock.
Who's there?
Israel.
Israel who?
Israel happy to see you.

Knock, knock.
Who's there?
Jet.
Jet who?
Jet little ol' me.

Knock, knock.
Who's there?
Lux.
Lux who?
Lux like we're locked out of the house.

Knock, knock.
Who's there?
Michelle.
Michelle who?
Michelle with the other shells down by the seashore.

Knock, knock.
Who's there?
Ocelot.
Ocelot who?
Ocelot of questions, don't you?

Knock, knock.
Who's there?
Spell.
Spell who?
W-h-o.

Knock, knock.
Who's there?
Tara.
Tara who?
Tara-ra boom-de-ay!

Knock, knock.
Who's there?
Wooden Shoe.
Wooden Shoe who?
Wooden Shoe like to know?

17

THE DOORBELL IS BROKEN!

Knock, knock.
Who's there?
Anais.
Anais who?
Anais looking door you have there.

Knock, knock.
Who's there?
Carrie.
Carrie who?
"Carrie me back to old Virginny…"

Knock, knock.
Who's there?
Doughnut.
Doughnut who?
Doughnut close the door—my foot is in it!

Knock, knock.
Who's there?
Elizabeth.
Elizabeth who?
Elizabeth of knowledge is a dangerous thing.

Knock, knock.
Who's there?
Groom.
Groom who?
There's plenty of Groom for more.

Knock, knock.
Who's there?
Honeydew.
Honeydew who?
Honeydew you want to go on a date?

Knock, knock.
Who's there?
Ida.
Ida who?
Ida know, do you?

Knock, knock.
Who's there?
Lovitt.
Lovitt who?
Lovitt or leave it.

Knock, knock.
Who's there?
Odette.
Odette who?
Odette's a bad sign when you can't remember my name!

Knock, knock.
Who's there?
Police.
Police who?
Police don't make me stand out here.

Knock, knock.
Who's there?
Tarzan.
Tarzan who?
Tarzan stripes forever!

Knock, knock.
Who's there?
Wendy.
Wendy who?
Wendy joke is over, you had better laugh.

18

NOBODY'S HOME!

Knock, knock.
Who's there?
Ben.
Ben who?
Ben here a while—want to let me in?

Knock, knock.
Who's there?
Caesars.
Caesars who?
Caesars help you cut things.

Knock, knock.
Who's there?
Doris.
Doris who?
Doris open—may I come in?

Knock, knock.
Who's there?
Emma.
Emma who?
Emma in town now, how about you?

Knock, knock.
Who's there?
Gideon.
Gideon who?
"Gideon up" is what you say to horses.

Knock, knock,
Who's there?
Hootie.
Hootie who?
Hootie you think is knocking on the door?

Knock, knock.
Who's there?
Karsen.
Karsen who?
Karsen the parking lot. Do you have the keys?

Knock, knock.
Who's there?
Martian.
Martian who?
Martian around in front of your house makes me tired.

Knock, knock.
Who's there?
Oscar.
Oscar who?
Oscar silly question, get a silly answer.

Knock, knock.
Who's there?
Passion.
Passion who?
Passion cars on a busy road can be dangerous.

Knock, knock.
Who's there?
Suture.
Suture who?
Suture self—I'll knock on someone else's door.

Knock, knock.
Who's there?
Teacher.
Teacher who?
That'll Teacher to knock on my door in the middle of
   the night!

Knock, knock.
Who's there?
Walter.
Walter who?
Walter you waiting for?

19

RAP, RAP, RAP!

Knock, knock.
Who's there?
Abby.
Abby who?
Abby stung me.

Knock, knock.
Who's there?
Bridie.
Bridie who?
I found my way Bridie light of my flashlight.

Knock, knock.
Who's there?
Carmen.
Carmen who?
Carmen get it!

Knock, knock.
Who's there?
Elsie.
Elsie who?
Elsie you tomorrow—I'm getting tired of waiting.

Knock, knock.
Who's there?
Godiva.
Godiva who?
Godiva in the swimming pool.

Knock, knock.
Who's there?
Into.
Into who?
Into minutes you'll be in trouble if you don't let me in.

Knock, knock.
Who's there?
Kerri.
Kerri who?
Kerri my backpack, will you?

Knock, knock.
Who's there?
Locker.
Locker who?
Locker out of the house!

Knock, knock.
Who's there?
Major.
Major who?
Major open the door, didn't I!

Knock, knock.
Who's there?
Owl.
Owl who?
Owl see you later.

Knock, knock.
Who's there?
Peace.
Peace who?
Peace don't tell me any more knock-knock jokes.

Knock, knock.
Who's there?
Teheran.
Teheran who?
Teheran away!

Knock, knock.
Who's there?
Willa.
Willa who?
Willa 'nother joke get you to open the door?

20

GO AWAY!

Knock, knock.
Who's there?
Arthur.
Arthur who?
Arthur any kids who want to come out and play?

Knock, knock.
Who's there?
Boyd.
Boyd who?
Boyd, I wish I had more knock-knock jokes!

Knock, knock.
Who's there?
Cashew.
Cashew who?
Cashew see I'm freezing out here?

Knock, knock.
Who's there?
Donna.
Donna who?
Donna you know? Open the door and see.

Knock, knock.
Who's there?
Fanny.
Fanny who?
Fanny knock-knock joke, isn't it?

Knock, knock.
Who's there?
Gus.
Gus who?
Gus whose coming for dinner?

Knock, knock.
Who's there?
Howdy.
Howdy who?
Howdy get in there?

Knock, knock.
Who's there?
I Wish.
I Wish who?
My dog—an I Wish setter.

Knock, knock.
Who's there?
Kook.
Kook who?
What are you, a clock?

Knock, knock.
Who's there?
L.B.
L.B. who?
L.B. seeing you later.

Knock, knock.
Who's there?
Macron.
Macron who?
I'm Macron pancakes for breakfast.

Knock, knock.
Who's there?
Papa.
Papa who?
Papa goes the weasel.

Knock, knock.
Who's there?
Sherbet.
Sherbet who?
Sherbet you'd love to hear some more jokes.

Knock, knock.
Who's there?
Theresa.
Theresa who?
Theresa green and the sky is blue.

Knock, knock.
Who's there?
Winnie.
Winnie who?
Winnie hear a knock-knock joke, I start laughing.

21

ANYBODY HOME?

Knock, knock.
Who's there?
Anthem.
Anthem who?
You Anthem devil, you!

Knock, knock.
Who's there?
Butter.
Butter who?
Butter open the door!

Knock, knock.
Who's there?
Cello.
Cello who?
Cello, how are you?

Knock, knock.
Who's there?
Dublin.
Dublin who?
Dublin over with laughter at these knock-knock jokes.

Knock, knock.
Who's there?
Flora.
Flora who?
I'm rolling on the Flora laughing.

Knock, knock.
Who's there?
Giraffe.
Giraffe who?
Tom Sawyer floated the Mississippi on Giraffe.

Knock, knock.
Who's there?
Huron.
Huron who?
Huron my foot—please get off!

Knock, knock.
Who's there?
Jaws.
Jaws who?
Jaws for fun.

Knock, knock.
Who's there?
Kurt C.
Kurt C. who?
Kurt C. is what polite girls do.

Knock, knock.
Who's there?
Len.
Len who?
Len me five bucks, would ya?

Knock, knock.
Who's there?
Napkin.
Napkin who?
A Napkin help you out when you are tired.

Knock, knock.
Who's there?
Osborn.
Osborn who?
Osborn in Wisconsin. Where were you born?

Knock, knock.
Who's there?
Polyp.
Polyp who?
Polyp a chair and sit down.

Knock, knock.
Who's there?
Saber.
Saber who?
Saber strength and rest awhile.

Knock, knock.
Who's there?
Thesis.
Thesis who?
Thesis almost the end of the jokes.

Knock, knock.
Who's there?
Tilly.
Tilly who?
Tilly opens the door, I'll keep knocking.

Knock, knock.
Who's there?
Watson.
Watson who?
Watson television?

Knock, knock.
Who's there?
Rick Ord.
Rick Ord who?
Rick Ord the show for me tonight, please.

Knock, knock.
Who's there?
Hogwash.
Hogwash who?
Hogwash Charlie—I'll clean your Harley.

Knock, knock.
Who's there?
Kitty Litter.
Kitty Litter who?
Will the Kitty Litter kittens come out to play?

Knock, knock.
Who's there?
Slipper.
Slipper who?
Slipper foot into the shoe to see if it fits.

Knock, knock.
Who's there?
Jacket.
Jacket who?
Jacket the door—let me in!

Knock, knock.
Who's there?
Faucet.
Faucet who?
Let's watch *The Wizard of Faucet* your house!

Knock, knock.
Who's there?
Pike.
Pike who?
Pike's peeking in your window.

Knock, knock.
Who's there?
Jess.
Jess who?
I Jess got here a minute late.

Knock, knock.
Who's there?
Lightning.
Lightning who?
Lightning this campfire is hard!

Knock, knock.
Who's there?
Ben.
Ben who?
Ben getting tired of standing outside.

Knock, knock.
Who's there?
Disguise.
Disguise who?
Disguise pretty funny, isn't he?

Knock, knock.
Who's there?
Flora.
Flora who?
Flora my house got wet when the water pipe burst.

Knock, knock.
Who's there?
Goliath.
Goliath who?
Goliath down and take a nap.

Knock, knock.
Who's there?
Hank.
Hank who?
Hank you for finally opening the door.

Knock, knock.
Who's there?
Isaiah.
Isaiah who?
Isaiah it again: I'd like to come in.

Knock, knock.
Who's there?
Jeer.
Jeer who?
Jeer about the chicken that crossed the road?
  He wanted to get to the other side.

Knock, knock.
Who's there?
Landon.
Landon who?
Landon on your bottom doesn't feel good.

Knock, knock.
Who's there?
Milton.
Milton who?
Milton my ice-cream cone, waiting for you to open the
  door.

Knock, knock.
Who's there?
Phillip.
Phillip who?
Phillip your piggy bank with money.

Knock, knock.
Who's there?
Queen.
Queen who?
Queen up your act and open the door!

Knock, knock.
Who's there?
Snapper.
Snapper who?
Snapper fingers and I'll come running.

Knock, knock.
Who's there?
Theodore.
Theodore who?
Theodore is closed. Open up!

Knock, knock.
Who's there?
Violet.
Violet who?
Violet the cat out of the bag.

Knock, knock.
Who's there?
Weed.
Weed who?
Weed better stop telling these knock-knock jokes, or
we'll run out.

Knock, knock.
Who's there?
Yah.
Yah who?
What are you so excited about?

Knock, knock.
Who's there?
Annapolis.
Annapolis who?
Annapolis a great snack.

Knock, knock.
Who's there?
Beacon.
Beacon who?
That Beacon sting you—watch out!

Knock, knock.
Who's there?
Everett.
Everett who?
Everett a lizard before?

Knock, knock.
Who's there?
Far East.
Far East who?
Far East a jolly good fellow . . .

Knock, knock.
Who's there?
Gomez.
Gomez who?
I don't know—he left to wash his face and Gomez hair.

Knock, knock.
Who's there?
Italia.
Italia who?
Italia if you really want to know.

Knock, knock.
Who's there?
Jerky.
Jerky who?
Jerky work in the lock? Mine doesn't.

Knock, knock.
Who's there?
Keanu.
Keanu who?
Keanu hear me knocking?

Knock, knock.
Who's there?
Leda.
Leda who?
Leda me to the back door—maybe it's open.

Knock, knock.
Who's there?
Morrie.
Morrie who?
The Morrie knock-knock jokes I read, the sillier they get.

Knock, knock.
Who's there?
Oil.
Oil who?
Oil tell you when you open the door.

Knock, knock.
Who's there?
Phyllis.
Phyllis who?
Phyllis in on the latest news.

Knock, knock.
Who's there?
Queue.
Queue who?
Queue come quick and open the door!

Knock, knock.
Who's there?
Raymond.
Raymond who?
Raymond me to get another joke book!

Knock, knock.
Who's there?
Sandy.
Sandy who?
Sandy Claus—he's coming to town.

Knock, knock.
Who's there?
Weird.
Weird who?
Weird you hear that joke?

Knock, knock.
Who's there?
Yule.
Yule who?
Yule see if you open the door.

Knock, knock.
Who's there?
Baker.
Baker who?
Baker a cake—it's her birthday!

Knock, knock.
Who's there?
Cereal.
Cereal who?
Cereal nice of you to open the door.

Knock, knock.
Who's there?
Denise.
Denise who?
Denise are sore from playing marbles.

Knock, knock.
Who's there?
Dismay.
Dismay who?
Dismay be my last knock-knock joke.